Contents

How to use this book

Each page has a title telling you what it is about.

Instructions look like this. Always read these carefully before starting.

This shows you how to set out your work. The first question is done for you.

Ask your teacher if you need to do these.

Read these word problems very carefully. Decide how you will work out the answers.

Sometimes there is a **Hint** to help you.

Sometimes you need materials to help you.

Counters

This shows that the activity is an **Explore**. Work with a friend.

This means you decide how to set out your work.

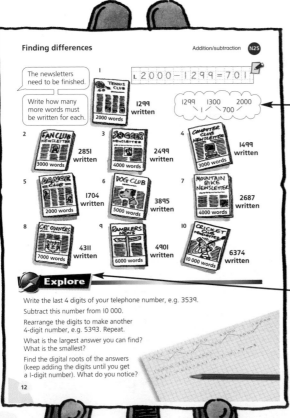

Adding multiples of 10 and 100

Write how high each cliff is.

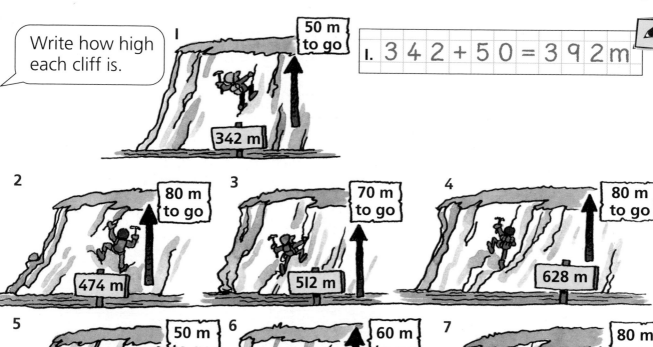

1. 50 m to go / 342 m

$$I.\ 3\ 4\ 2\ +\ 5\ 0\ =\ 3\ 9\ 2\ m$$

2. 80 m to go / 474 m

3. 70 m to go / 512 m

4. 80 m to go / 628 m

5. 50 m to go / 394 m

6. 60 m to go / 728 m

7. 80 m to go / 881 m

8. 60 m to go / 353 m

9. 60 m to go / 466 m

10. 50 m to go / 575 m

e Each climber has already climbed 50 m. Where did they start?

Copy and complete.

11. $342 + 400 =$

$$II.\ 3\ 4\ 2\ +\ 4\ 0\ 0\ =\ 7\ 4\ 2$$

12. $612 + 200 =$

13. $568 + \underline{} = 1068$

14. $736 + \underline{} = 1136$

15. $827 + 700 =$

16. $447 + 600 =$

17. $\underline{} + 800 = 1389$

3

Subtracting multiples of 10 and 100

Each shop sells some stock.

Write how many items are left.

1 TEDDY BEARS

325 sell 60

1. $325 - 60 = 265$

2 TOY CARS

142 sell 50

3 ROBOTS

241 sell 80

4 LAMPS

304 sell 90

5 BALLS

519 sell 40

6 SANDWICHES

457 sell 70

7 SHOES

112 sell 30

8 TOOLS

421 sell 60

9 HATS

638 sell 90

10 BOOKS

803 sell 20

e The next day each shop gets a delivery of 40 items. Write how much stock each has now.

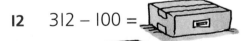

Copy and complete.

11. $465 - 200 = 265$

11 $465 - 200 =$

12 $312 - 100 =$

13 $672 - \square = 372$

14 $702 - \square = 302$

15 $\square - 200 = 313$

16 $440 - 150 =$

17 $724 - 230 =$

18 $620 - \square = 150$

4

Adding 2-digit and 3-digit numbers

Forest rangers are planting trees.

Write how many trees are in each forest.

1

117

24 planted

I. $117 + 24 = 141$

2

247

62 planted

3

333

74 planted

4

109

68 planted

5

224

46 planted

6

345

73 planted

7

472

46 planted

8

529

82 planted

9

668

55 planted

10

981

37 planted

☻ A hurricane blows down 34 trees in each forest. Write how many trees there are now.

11 Melissa is paid **£248** each week.

£248

She spends **£64** on rent and **£21** on bills.

How much money does she have left?

Problems

12 Wesley swims **48 m**.

He has a rest then swims another **146 m**.

His trainer says he must swim **300 m**. How much further must Wesley swim?

5

The trains stop at a station.

Write how many passengers are left on each train.

1. $582 - 74 = 508$

1   **582 passengers**

74 get off

2   **475 passengers**

82 get off

3   **366 passengers**

71 get off

4   **251 passengers**

48 get off

5   **388 passengers**

69 get off

6   **219 passengers**

44 get off

7   **504 passengers**

28 get off

8   **399 passengers**

52 get off

9   **484 passengers**

85 get off

10   **527 passengers**

72 get off

e   At the next station 46 people get on. Write how many passengers on each train now.

Explore

Use number cards 0 to 9.

Make five 2-digit numbers.

Start with 300. Subtract all five numbers and write down the final answer.

What is the smallest answer you can find?

Which numbers give the answer nearest to 100?

Adding near multiples of 100

Write the new number.

1.

8 7 6

4 0 0 more

1. 8 7 6 + 4 0 0 = 1 2 7 6

2.

7 5 2

3 0 0 more

3.

5 9 2

2 0 0 more

4.

6 0 1

5 0 0 more

5.

4 8 3

7 0 0 more

6.

7 4 7

6 0 0 more

7.

3 6 9

8 0 0 more

℮ Subtract 400 from each new number.

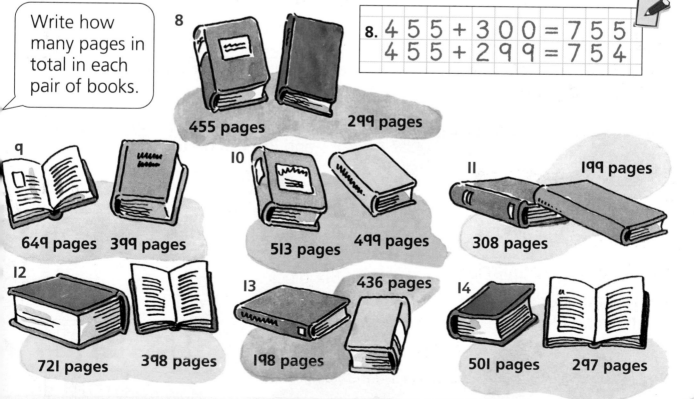

Write how many pages in total in each pair of books.

8

8. 4 5 5 + 3 0 0 = 7 5 5
   4 5 5 + 2 9 9 = 7 5 4

455 pages   299 pages

9
649 pages   399 pages

10
513 pages   499 pages

11
199 pages
308 pages

12
721 pages   398 pages

13
436 pages
198 pages

14
501 pages   297 pages

℮ Write the difference between the number of pages for each pair.

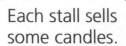

1 CANDLES

1. $385 - 199 = 186$

385 sell 199

2
273 sell 98

3
196 sell 99

4
364 sell 198

5
558 sell 203

6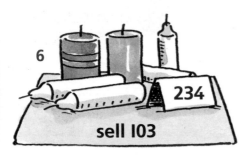
234 sell 103

7
381 sell 197

8
476 sell 299

2 Each stall sells 97 more candles. Write how many are left now.

Problems

9 The Wilde family go on holiday.

They drive for **3 days** to get there.

They drive **249 km** on the first day. On the second day they drive **349 km**, and **201 km** on the last day.

How far have they travelled?

10 Jamal and Shamilla are making models using building blocks.

There are **512** blocks in the box. Jamal uses **102**. Shamilla uses **299**.

How many blocks are left in the box?

Write how many of each computer game the shop has.

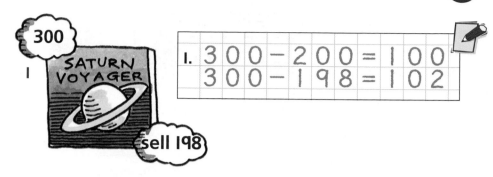

300
SATURN VOYAGER
sell 198

1. $300 - 200 = 100$
   $300 - 198 = 102$

420
BUNNY HOP
2
deliver 197

535
RACE 2000
3
sell 299

617
KERPOW!!
4
sell 198

724
WORLD TEAM TENNIS
5
deliver 209

856
STARSHOT
6
sell 397

965
SNAKE BYTE III
7
deliver 108

Explore

Write additions and subtractions using near multiples of 100, e.g.

$521 + 199 = 720$
$521 - 199 = 322$

Find the digital root of each number and the answers.

What do you notice? Is this always true?

Explore for additions and subtractions of other 3-digit numbers.

To find a **digital root**, add the digits of the number together. Keep adding until you get a 1-digit number.

$99 \rightarrow 9 + 9 = 18 \rightarrow 1 + 8 = \mathbf{9}$

Copy and complete.

> 1. $842 - 700 = 142$

1. $842 - 700$
2. $964 - 900$
3. $302 - 200$
4. $412 - 400$
5. $551 - 400$
6. $737 - 600$
7. $483 - 300$
8. $887 - 800$
9. $1043 - 900$

Write the difference between the cost of each pair of holidays.

10. Spain £405 / Greece £395

> 10. $£405 - £395 = £10$

11. Morocco £807 / Tunisia £796

12. Sicily £612 / Corsica £596

13. Ireland £210 / Wales £189

14. Italy £287 / France £302

15. New York £491 / Los Angeles £513

16. Australia £889 / New Zealand £905

17. Hong Kong £990 / Japan £1009

18. Poland £198 / Czech Republic £204

19. Egypt £689 / Kenya £711

e A holiday in the Caribbean costs £1020. Write how much more than the other holidays it costs.

Write how much more each plane needs for a full tank.

1. $3000 l - 1899 l = 1101 l$

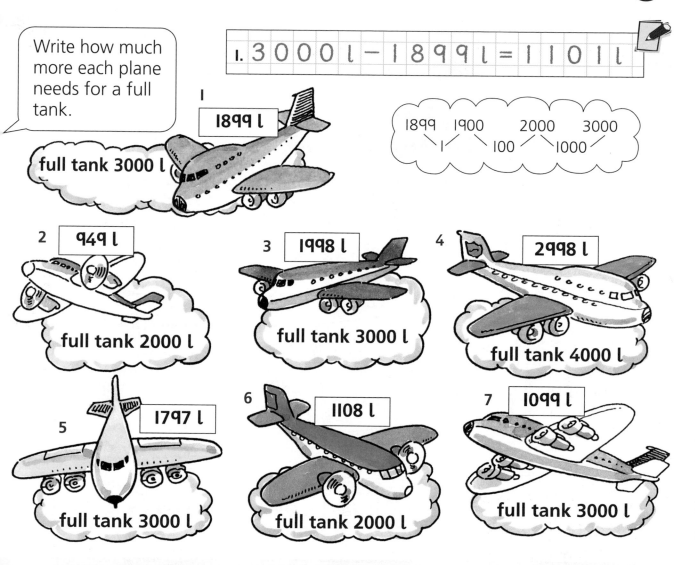

1899   1900   2000   3000
\ 1 /   \ 100 /   \ 1000 /

1   1899 l   full tank 3000 l

2   949 l   full tank 2000 l

3   1998 l   full tank 3000 l

4   2998 l   full tank 4000 l

5   1797 l   full tank 3000 l

6   1108 l   full tank 2000 l

7   1099 l   full tank 3000 l

Each plane uses 599 l of the fuel in its tank. Write how much fuel each plane has now.

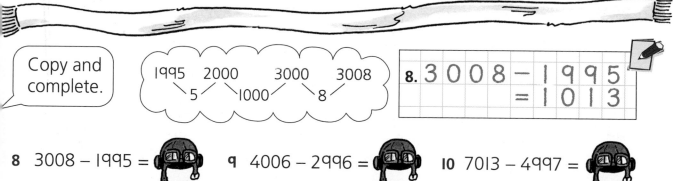

Copy and complete.

1995   2000   3000   3008
\ 5 /   \ 1000 /   \ 8 /

8. $3008 - 1995 = 1013$

8   $3008 - 1995 =$

9   $4006 - 2996 =$

10   $7013 - 4997 =$

11   $9004 - 8987 =$

12   $1042 - 899 =$

13   $8031 - 5995 =$

14   $5107 - 2992 =$

15   $6090 - 3991 =$

16   $3123 - 1989 =$

Finding differences

> The newsletters need to be finished.

> Write how many more words must be written for each.

1

TENNIS CLUB

1299 written

2000 words

1. $2000 - 1299 = 701$

1299   1300   2000
    \ 1 /   \ 700 /

2

FAN CLUB NEWSLETTER

2851 written

3000 words

3

SOCCER NEWSLETTER

2499 written

4000 words

4

COMPUTER CLUB NEWSLETTER

1499 written

3000 words

5

DANCE CLUB

1704 written

2000 words

6

DOG CLUB

3895 written

5000 words

7

MOUNTAIN BIKE NEWSLETTER

2687 written

4000 words

8

CAT OWNERS

4311 written

7000 words

9

RAMBLERS NEWS

4901 written

6000 words

10

CRICKET CLUB NEWSLETTER

6374 written

10 000 words

Explore

Write the last 4 digits of your telephone number, e.g. 3539.

Subtract this number from 10 000.

Rearrange the digits to make another 4-digit number, e.g. 5393. Repeat.

What is the largest answer you can find? What is the smallest?

Find the digital roots of the answers (keep adding the digits until you get a 1-digit number). What do you notice?

Subtracting 3-digit from 4-digit numbers

Copy and complete.

```
1    3 2 4 2
   -   8 8 6
   _____
```

```
1.   2 0 0 0

     3 2 4 2
   -   8 8 6
   _____
     2 3 5 6
```

```
2    4 6 3 1
   -   9 7 5
   _____
```

```
3    4 8 2 6
   -   9 3 7
   _____
```

```
4    5 7 1 4
   -   8 2 6
   _____
```

```
5    2 3 9 8
   -   9 9 9
   _____
```

```
6    6 1 4 9
   -   7 6 2
   _____
```

```
7    7 3 1 1
   -   5 3 4
   _____
```

```
8    9 0 3 6
   -   2 7 9
   _____
```

Each bookshop checks its stock at the end of the month.

Write how many books are left.

9   THE BOOK SHOP

4638 books
749 sold

```
9.   4 0 0 0

     4 6 3 8
   -   7 4 9
   _____
     3 8 8 9
```

10   BOOK NOOK

5217 books
698 sold

11   Books Books Books

3681 books
907 sold

12   BOOKWORM

2846 books
958 sold

13   PAGES

7013 books
826 sold

14   LOOK AT A BOOK

6955 books
768 sold

15   CHAPTER & VERSE

5241 books
475 sold

Write how far each parachutist has fallen.

1 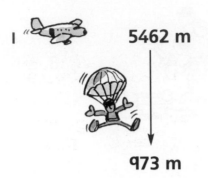 5462 m

973 m

1.
```
    4500
   ⁴5¹³4̶¹⁵6̶¹2 m
  −  9 7 3
    4 4 8 9
```

2 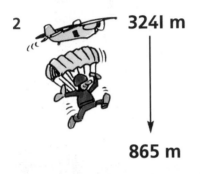 3241 m

865 m

3 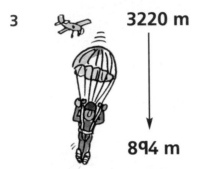 3220 m

894 m

4 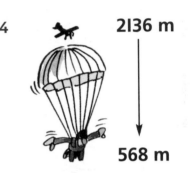 2136 m

568 m

5 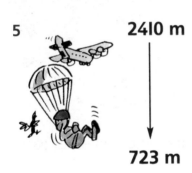 2410 m

723 m

6 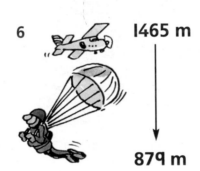 1465 m

879 m

7 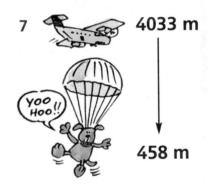 4033 m

458 m

Explore

Use number cards 2 to 8.

Make a 4-digit number and a 3-digit number.

Subtract the smaller number from the larger one.

Explore which pairs of numbers give answers nearest to 8000, 7500, 7000, 6500, …

Write the differences between the children's guesses and the actual number of sweets in the jars.

1  983

guess
1271

I.
$$\begin{array}{r} 300 \\ \cancel{1271} \\ -\ 983 \\ \hline 288 \end{array}$$

2  1524

guess
2461

3 1993

guess
3110

4  892

guess
1046

5  1189

guess
943

6  2417

guess
1973

7  1503

guess
1861

e The closest guess for each was 106 less than the actual total. Write the closest guess for each.

8 A record shop sells **£2467** of CDs in a week.

The staff wages are **£874**. The stock cost **£978**.

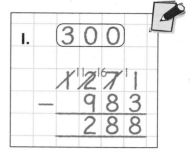

How much profit did the record shop make?

Problems

9 A plane is flying to Japan. The distance **9672 km** in total.

The plane lands after **1374 km** to pick up more passengers.

It stops again to refuel after another **3721 km**.

How much further is it to Japan?

JAPAN

Choosing strategies for mental subtractions

Subtract by counting on.

1. 3002 − 2750 = 252

1	3002 − 2750
2	4100 − 3501
3	5050 − 3897
4	1509 − 798
5	6006 − 4440
6	9013 − 7689
7	7401 − 6490
8	8069 − 7599

Subtract by rounding.

9. 400 − 199 = 201

9	400 − 199
10	1400 − 401
11	3200 − 299
12	1000 − 501
13	6600 − 799
14	7200 − 397
15	4100 − 898
16	5800 − 1002

Subtract by taking away.

17. 642 − 31 = 611

17	642 − 31
18	1374 − 42
19	415 − 7
20	628 − 21
21	1448 − 17
22	739 − 27
23	2019 − 12
24	4957 − 34

Choose how to subtract.

25	825 − 299
26	912 − 875
27	812 − 7
28	2007 − 1870
29	1184 − 14
30	1706 − 988
31	8400 − 699
32	2414 − 6

Choosing a strategy

1

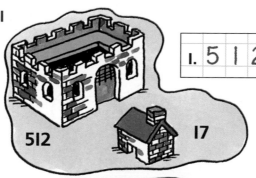

Write how many more bricks in the larger model.

Write which method you use.

512   17

$$1. \; 5\;1\;2\;-\;1\;7\;=\;4\;9\;5$$

2

99   342

3

635
551

4

318
497

5

678
125

6

506
297

7

1008
893

8

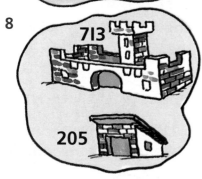

713
205

9

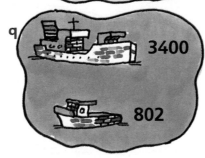

3400
802

10

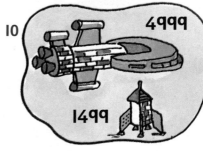

4999
1499

e Make up some subtractions where the larger model has 199 more bricks than the smaller one.

Explore

Use the number cards shown.

Use all the cards to make subtractions.

Find:

- the smallest possible answer
- the largest possible answer
- the answer nearest to 1000.

6 7 8 9 0

6780 – 9 =

Choosing a strategy

Write the number of years between each event.

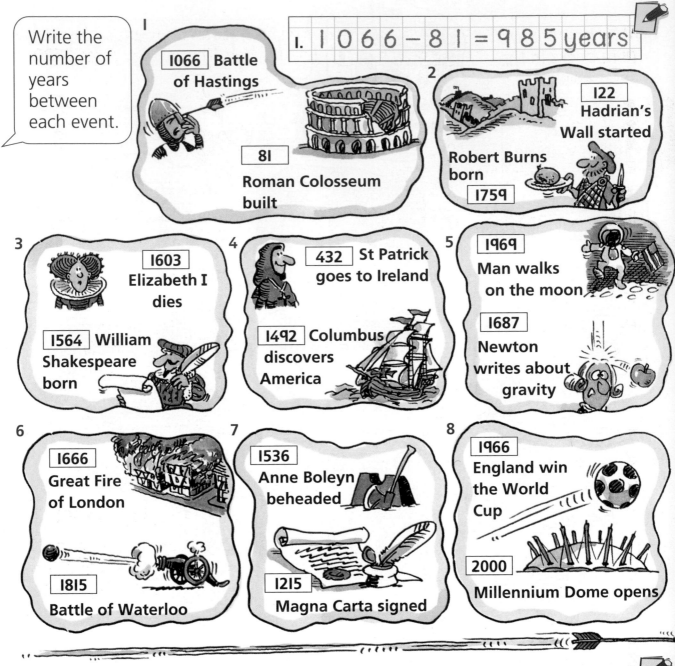

1. 1066 − 81 = 985 years

1
1066 Battle of Hastings
81 Roman Colosseum built

2
122 Hadrian's Wall started
Robert Burns born
1759

3
1603 Elizabeth I dies
1564 William Shakespeare born

4
432 St Patrick goes to Ireland
1492 Columbus discovers America

5
1969 Man walks on the moon
1687 Newton writes about gravity

6
1666 Great Fire of London
1815 Battle of Waterloo

7
1536 Anne Boleyn beheaded
1215 Magna Carta signed

8
1966 England win the World Cup
2000 Millennium Dome opens

Copy and complete.

9 4012 − 3997

9. 4012 − 3997 = 15

10 5674 − 32

11 1645 − 399

12 1246 − 998

13 7011 − 804

14 9283 − 6142

15 8760 − 480

16 6000 − 3118

17 4751 − 12

ℯ Write a matching addition for each.

Subtraction problems

1 There are **1248** people at the pantomime.

795 are children. How many are adults?

35 adults are asleep. How many are awake?

2 The Thomson family are saving to go on holiday. The holiday costs **£1120**.

They have saved **£675**.

How much more do they need?

3 Herbie is driving to Monte Carlo.

He has done **401 km**.

It is **1112 km** to Monte Carlo.

How much further must Herbie go to reach halfway?

4 Surrinder's dad wants to buy a car. He has **£1000**.

He buys a second-hand car for **£899**. How much does he have left?

5 Jake is buying a new computer. The computer costs **£699**.

Jake has **£301**.

How much does he need to borrow from his parents?

6 A lorry weighs **1120 kg**.

The bridge can only hold **750 kg**.

Each box on the lorry weighs **15 kg**.

How many boxes must be unloaded for the lorry to cross the bridge?

19

Divisibility tests

Some schools are playing in a tennis competition.

They play singles matches.

Find if all the children can play.

> 1. 3 4 4 → even
> 3 4 4 divides by 2
> yes, they can all play

1	344	2	261	3	110	4	332
5	1002	6	710	7	881	8	1040
9	2000	10	201	11	1066	12	9096
13	792	14	4056	15	1081	16	9090
17	4554	18	10 000	19	20 000	20	645
21	449	22	1036	23	2918	24	4040

Find if all the children can play in doubles matches.

> 1a. 3 4 4 ÷ 2 = 1 7 2
> 1 7 2 → even
> 3 4 4 divides by 4
> yes, they can all play

Divisibility tests

Write which numbers divide by 5 and which divide by 10.

1. 3 4 0 divides by 5 and by 1 0

1	340		**2**	725	

3	500	**4**	6005	**5**	75	
6	1000	**7**	6250	**8**	225	**9** 3500
10	7015	**11**	1505	**12**	2890	**13** 4300

Write which numbers divide by 100.

3a. 5 0 0 divides by 1 0 0

Leap years are divisible by 4.   Find if these are leap years.   Write 'yes' or 'no'.

14. no

14  1962

15  2012

16  1857

17  1768

18  1524

19 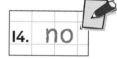 2082

20  1066

21 1662

22  2028

22

Divisibility tests

> Bouncy balls are packed in tubes of 2, 4, 5 or 10.

> Write which tubes each set of balls can be packed in.

1. 6 8 0 divides by 2, 4, 5 and 1 0

1 680	2 60	3 320	4 555	5 270
6 1000	7 900	8 305	9 999	10 348
11 770	12 504	13 6060	14 7000	15 1515

e Write which sets of balls could be packed in tubes of 8.

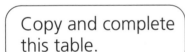

> Copy and complete this table.

	÷ 2	÷ 4	÷ 5	÷ 10	÷ 100
60	✔	✔	✔	✔	✘
720					
945					
300					
7644					
1000					
258					

Factors

Write the missing numbers.

I. $10 = 1 \times 10, \ 2 \times 5$

1 $10 = 1 \times \bigcirc, \ 2 \times \bigcirc$

2 $14 = 1 \times \bigcirc, \ 2 \times \bigcirc$

3 $16 = 1 \times \bigcirc, \ 2 \times \bigcirc, \ 4 \times \bigcirc$

4 $21 = 1 \times \bigcirc, \ 3 \times \bigcirc$

5 $35 = 1 \times \bigcirc, \ 5 \times \bigcirc$

6 $42 = 1 \times \bigcirc, \ 2 \times \bigcirc, \ 3 \times \bigcirc, \ 6 \times \bigcirc$

7 $48 = 1 \times \bigcirc, \ 2 \times \bigcirc, \ 3 \times \bigcirc, \ 4 \times \bigcirc, \ 6 \times \bigcirc$

8 $60 = 1 \times \bigcirc, \ 2 \times \bigcirc, \ 3 \times \bigcirc, \ 4 \times \bigcirc, \ 5 \times \bigcirc, \ 6 \times \bigcirc$

9 $25 = 1 \times \bigcirc, \ 5 \times \bigcirc$

10 $18 = 1 \times \bigcirc, \ 2 \times \bigcirc, \ 3 \times \bigcirc$

List all the factors of each number in order.

Ia. factors of 1 0: 1, 2, 5, 1 0

Write all the different pairs of factors for each number.

11 12

II. $1 \times 1 2, \ 2 \times 6, \ 3 \times 4$

12 24

13 32

14 36

15 28

16 30

17 40

18 45

19 50

20 23

21 49

List the factors of each number.

IIa. factors of 1 2: 1, 2, 3, 4, 6, 1 2

Factors

The cards show the factors of each number.

Write the missing factor.

1 12

3 1 ▨ 6 2 12

1. 4

2 16

4 ▨ 2
16 1

3 28

2 1 ▨
28 7 14

4 50

5 2 50
▨ 1 10

5 35

1 35
5 ▨

6 32

4 1 ▨
32 2 16

7 40

10 2 4 ▨
5 1 40 20

8 22

22 2
▨ 1

Which number from each list is not a factor of the star number?

9 24
8, 3, 6, 16

9. 16

10 36
3, 20, 12, 4

11 40
10, 4, 6, 2

12 50
2, 25, 15, 10

13 28
4, 6, 17, 7

14 32
2, 7, 16, 1

15 54
18, 7, 3, 2

16 56
14, 9, 7, 4

17 500
3, 10, 5, 2

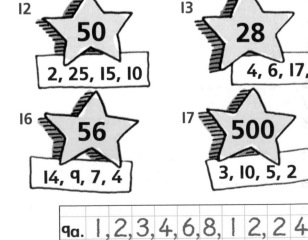

Write all the factors of each star number.

9a. 1, 2, 3, 4, 6, 8, 12, 24

Factors

These are pairs of factors.

Write the missing numbers.

I. $4 \times 8 = 2 \times 16$

1   $4 \times 8 = \bigcirc \times 16$

2   $\bigcirc \times 10 = 4 \times 5$

3   $2 \times 8 = \bigcirc \times 4$

4   $3 \times 8 = \bigcirc \times 4$

5   $5 \times \bigcirc = 3 \times 10$

6   $2 \times 21 = \bigcirc \times 7$

7   $3 \times 12 = 6 \times \bigcirc$

8   $2 \times 25 = \bigcirc \times 10$

9   $3 \times \bigcirc = 6 \times 10$

10   $8 \times 8 = \bigcirc \times 16$

Copy and complete the table.

Write the factors of numbers up to 40.

Number	Pairs of factors	List of factors
1	1×1	1
2	1×2	1, 2
3	1×3	1, 3
4	$1 \times 4, 2 \times 2$	1, 2, 4

Explore

4 has three factors: 1, 2 and 4.

16 has five factors: 1, 2, 4, 8 and 16.

Explore other numbers which have an odd number of factors. What do you notice about them?

Use the table above to help you.

Negative numbers

Write the position of each arrow.

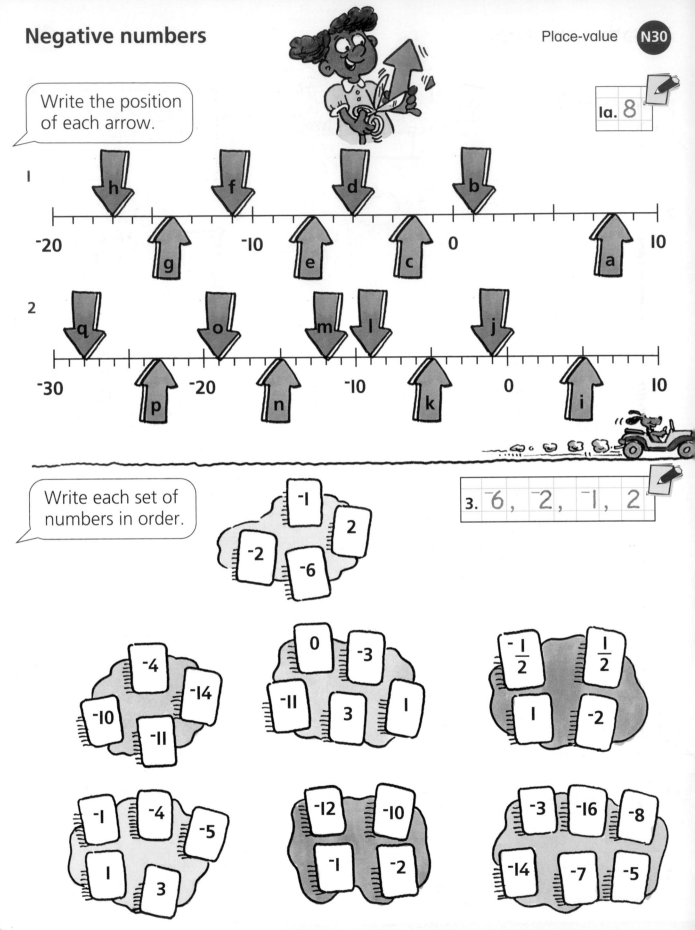

Write each set of numbers in order.

3. $^-6$, $^-2$, $^-1$, 2

e Draw a number line and mark all these numbers on it.

Negative numbers

Write how much each child has.

1. Clare owes £30  £25

I.	has	£ 2 5		
	owes	£ 3 0		
	total	= ⁻£ 5		

2. Jon owes £25  £10

3. Layla owes £32  £30

4. Dev owes £101 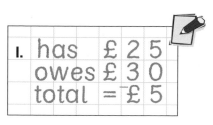 £100

5. Marie owes £21  £17

6. Paul owes £49  £42

7. Natalie owes £32  £26

8. Dion owes £70  £67

9. Marta owes £69  £53

10. Jamie owes £88 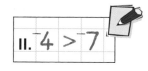 £74

e Each child borrows another £5. Write the new totals.

Write < or > between each pair of numbers.

11 ⁻4 ⬭ ⁻7

12 ⁻1 ⬭ ⁻10

II.	⁻4 > ⁻7

Use a number line to help you.

13 ⁻0·5 ⬭ ⁻0·7

14 ⁻6 ⬭ ⁻3

15 ⁻$\frac{1}{2}$ ⬭ ⁻$\frac{3}{4}$

16 ⁻2 ⬭ 1

17 ⁻5 ⬭ 0·5

18 ⁻$\frac{1}{2}$ ⬭ ⁻2

19 ⁻6 ⬭ 4

27

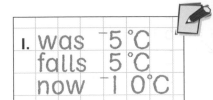

Each morning in the winter holiday the temperature is ⁻5°C.

Write the temperature each afternoon.

1. was ⁻5°C
falls 5°C
now ⁻10°C

1 falls 5 °C

2  rises 2 °C

3  rises 7 °C

4  falls 3 °C

5  falls 9 °C

6  rises 5 °C

7  falls 1 °C

8  falls 11 °C

9 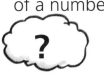 rises 10 °C

10 falls 8 °C

e At night each afternoon temperature falls by 7 °C. Write the temperature each night.

Problems

11 Marco owes his mum **£10**. His uncle sends him **£20** for his birthday.

He borrows some more money from his mum to pay his friend **£25** for a concert ticket.

How much does Marco owe his mum now?

12 Emily is thinking of a number.

 **?**

It is more than ⁻**10** but less than **0**.

It divides by **2** and by **3**.

What is Emily's number?

Copy and complete.

Estimate first.

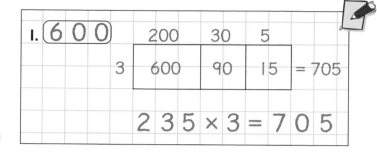

I.

	200	30	5	
3	600	90	15	= 705

$235 \times 3 = 705$

1 235×3

2 165×3

3 238×3

4 414×8

5 523×4

6 460×5

7 320×7

8 195×6

9 172×4

10 286×7

Jersey £144

Madrid £236

Orlando £358

Paris £109

Rome £283

Write the cost of these flights.

Estimate first. Use both methods.

11 **3 to Jersey**

12 **3 to Madrid**

13 **4 to Rome**

14 **3 to Orlando**

15 **7 to Madrid**

16 **8 to Paris**

17 **5 to Madrid**

18 **6 to Jersey**

19 **3 to Rome**

20 **6 to Orlando**

II.

a.

	100	40	4	
3	300	120	12	= 432

$£144 \times 3 = £432$

b.
```
  £ 1 4 4
  ×     3
      1 2     3 × 4
    1 2 0     3 × 40
    3 0 0     3 × 100
  £ 4 3 2
```

Multiplying by 1-digit numbers

Copy and complete.

Estimate first.

1
```
  4 2 7
×     3
───────
```

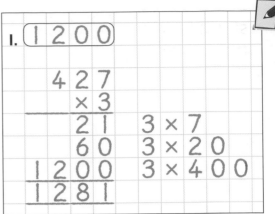

1.
```
┌─────────┐
│ 1 2 0 0 │
└─────────┘
    4 2 7
  ×     3
  ───────
      2 1    3 × 7
      6 0    3 × 2 0
  1 2 0 0    3 × 4 0 0
  ───────
  1 2 8 1
```

2
```
  1 2 8
×     3
───────
```

3
```
  3 1 5
×     4
───────
```

4
```
  2 5 4
×     5
───────
```

5
```
  3 3 3
×     4
───────
```

6
```
  5 2 0
×     5
───────
```

7
```
  4 0 6
×     6
───────
```

8
```
  7 0 3
×     6
───────
```

9
```
  1 5 1
×     7
───────
```

10
```
  2 6 8
×     8
───────
```

Write the capacity of 4 of each.

11  142 ml

II.
```
┌─────────┐
│ 6 0 0 ml │
└─────────┘
    1 4 2 ml
  ×     4
  ───────
        8    4 × 2
    1 6 0    4 × 4 0
    4 0 0    4 × 1 0 0
  ───────
    5 6 8 ml
```

12 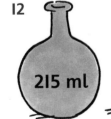 215 ml

13  173 ml

14 326 ml

15  412 ml

16 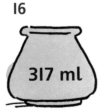 317 ml

17 284 ml

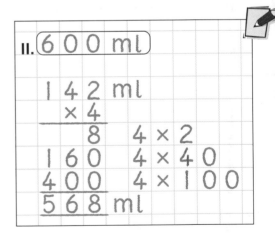

Write the capacity of 7 of each.

30

Multiplying by 2-digit numbers

> Estimate. Copy and complete.

1
```
   2 6
 × 1 4
 ─────
```

2
```
   3 4
 × 1 6
 ─────
```

3
```
   2 5
 × 1 3
 ─────
```

4
```
   2 8
 × 1 7
 ─────
```

5
```
   3 5
 × 1 9
 ─────
```

6
```
   4 6
 × 1 5
 ─────
```

7
```
   1 8
 × 2 7
 ─────
```

8
```
   3 2
 × 2 4
 ─────
```

9
```
   1 9
 × 2 6
 ─────
```

10
```
   6 3
 × 2 2
 ─────
```

11
```
   5 4
 × 3 1
 ─────
```

1. 300

a.

	20	6	
10	200	60	
4	80	24	= 364

$26 × 14 = 364$

b.
```
     2 6
   ×  1 4
   ─────
     2 4    4 × 6
     8 0    4 × 20
     6 0    10 × 6
   2 0 0    10 × 20
   ─────
   3 6 4
```

> Write how many people are in each audience.

12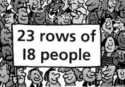
23 rows of 18 people

13
31 rows of 15 people

14
14 rows of 42 people

15
22 rows of 17 people

16
35 rows of 11 people

17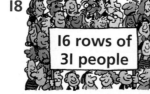
19 rows of 24 people

18
16 rows of 31 people

19
27 rows of 42 people

20
15 rows of 35 people

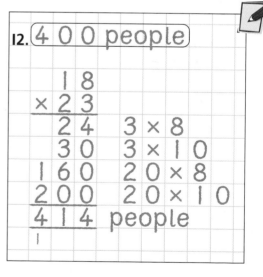

12. 400 people
```
       1 8
     × 2 3
     ─────
       2 4    3 × 8
       3 0    3 × 10
     1 6 0    20 × 8
     2 0 0    20 × 10
     ─────
     4 1 4    people
```

Multiplying by 2-digit numbers

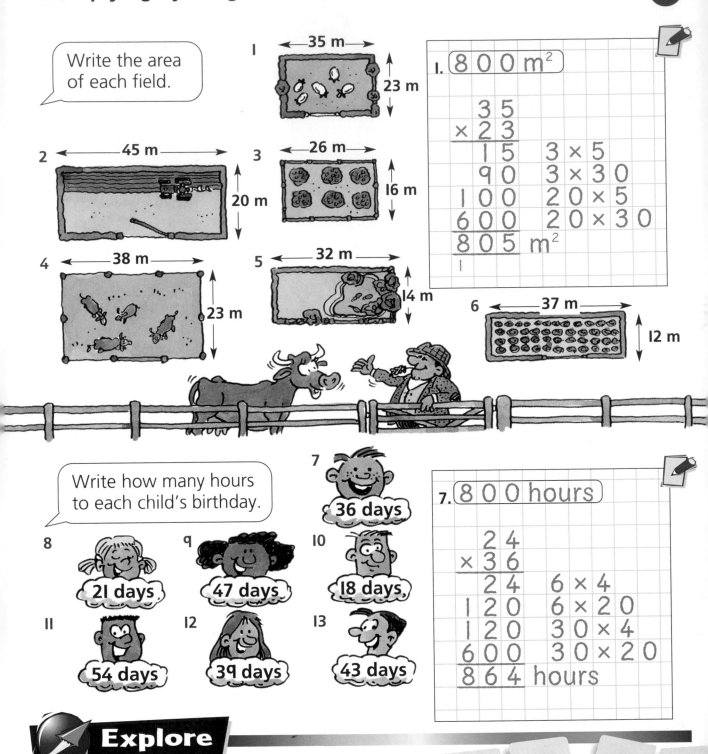

Write the area of each field.

1. 35 m × 23 m

2. 45 m × 20 m

3. 26 m × 16 m

4. 38 m × 23 m

5. 32 m × 14 m

6. 37 m × 12 m

1. 800 m²

```
    3 5
  × 2 3
    1 5    3 × 5
    9 0    3 × 3 0
  1 0 0    2 0 × 5
  6 0 0    2 0 × 3 0
  8 0 5    m²
  1
```

Write how many hours to each child's birthday.

7. 36 days

8. 21 days

9. 47 days

10. 18 days

11. 54 days

12. 39 days

13. 43 days

7. 800 hours

```
      2 4
    × 3 6
      2 4    6 × 4
    1 2 0    6 × 2 0
    1 2 0    3 0 × 4
    6 0 0    3 0 × 2 0
    8 6 4    hours
```

Explore

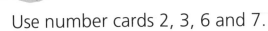

Use number cards 2, 3, 6 and 7.

Make two 2-digit numbers. Multiply them together.

Investigate different answers. Which is the largest?
Which is the smallest?

Multiplying decimals

Complete these multiplications.

I 5×2.4

I. **I O**

$5 \times 2.0 = I O.0$
$5 \times 0.4 = 2.0$
$5 \times 2.4 = I 2.0$

2 3×4.3 **3** 6×3.4 **4** 3×7.2

5 4×6.8 **6** 6×1.9 **7** 3×3.4 **8** 4×1.4

9 5×3.7 **10** 4×2.6 **II** 6×5.4 **12** 3×4.9

13 6×2.8 **14** 4×1.9 **15** 3×3.7 **16** 4×9.1

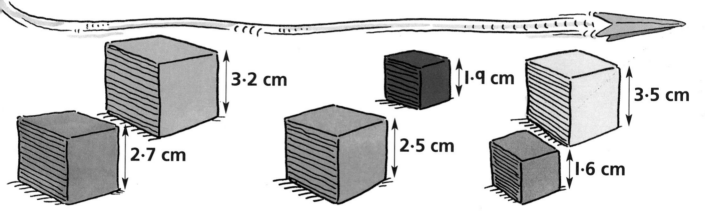

3.2 cm

1.9 cm

3.5 cm

2.7 cm

2.5 cm

1.6 cm

Write the heights of towers built with these cubes.

17 3 blue

18 4 red

17. **9 cm**

$3 \times 3.0 = 9.0$
$3 \times 0.2 = 0.6$
$3 \times 3.2 = 9.6$ cm

19 6 yellow **20** 5 pink

21 3 orange **22** 2 brown **23** 3 yellow **24** 2 red

25 3 pink **26** 4 brown **27** 5 blue **28** 6 orange

29 5 brown **30** 6 red **31** 4 orange **32** 9 blue

ℓ Write the height of a tower made with 3 cubes of each colour.

Multiplying decimals

1·6 cm   2·4 cm   1·8 cm   3·1 cm   1·3 cm   2·7 cm

Write the total width of:

1. 5 dictionaries

1. 15 cm

$$5 \times 3·0 = 15·0$$
$$5 \times 0·1 = 0·5$$
$$5 \times 3·1 = 15·5 \text{ cm}$$

2. 4 atlases

3. 3 computer guides

4. 2 joke books

5. 6 photo albums

6. 4 diaries

7. 3 atlases

8. 5 computer guides

9. 6 diaries

10. 5 joke books

11. 8 photo albums

12. 6 atlases

13. 7 joke books

14. 6 computer guides

15. 7 dictionaries

How long a shelf would be needed to hold 3 of all the books?

Complete these multiplications.

16. $3 \times 2·6 =$

17. $4 \times 1·8 =$

18. $2 \times 3·8 =$

19. $4 \times 5·6 =$

20. $6 \times 3·4 =$

21. $7 \times 1·9 =$

22. $8 \times 2·5 =$

23. $9 \times 3·7 =$

24. $4 \times 6·3 =$

25. $3 \times 11·2 =$

26. $2 \times 15·7 =$

Multiplying decimals

The floors of these rooms are regular polygons.

Write the perimeter of the floor of each room.

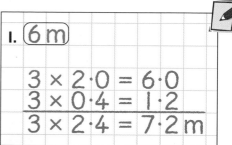

1. (6 m)

$3 \times 2 \cdot 0 = 6 \cdot 0$
$3 \times 0 \cdot 4 = 1 \cdot 2$
$3 \times 2 \cdot 4 = 7 \cdot 2$ m

1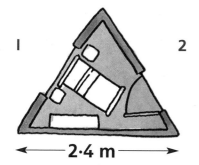
← 2·4 m →

2
← 3·2 m →

3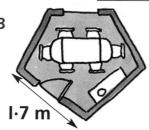
1·7 m

4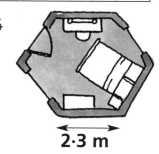
2·3 m

5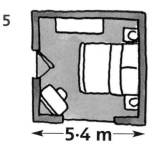
← 5·4 m →

6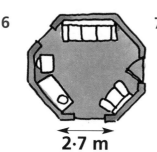
2·7 m

7
← 4·3 m →

8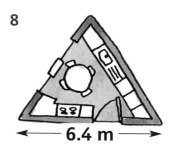
← 6·4 m →

9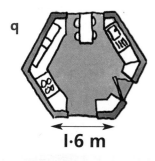
1·6 m

10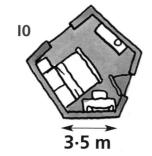
3·5 m

11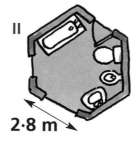
2·8 m

12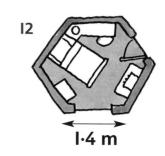
1·4 m

ℯ Write the perimeter of the floor of a room with 9 sides each 1·9 m long.

Complete these multiplications.

13 $4 \times 5 \cdot 3 =$

14 $5 \times 16 \cdot 2 =$

15 $3 \times 12 \cdot 7 =$

16 $4 \times 15 \cdot 4 =$

17 $7 \times 11 \cdot 8 =$

18 $8 \times 12 \cdot 6 =$

19 $3 \times 15 \cdot 2 =$

20 $5 \times 10 \cdot 7 =$

21 $4 \times 21 \cdot 3 =$

22 $6 \times 13 \cdot 8 =$

23 $7 \times 14 \cdot 3 =$

Write the weight of 9 of each.

1 CAT FOOD 3·2 kg

2 DOG FOOD 1·9 kg

$$1. \quad \boxed{2\,7\text{ kg}}$$
$$9 \times 3\cdot2 = 270 + 1\cdot8$$
$$= 28\cdot8 \text{ kg}$$

3 OSTRICH FOOD 4·3 kg

4 MOUSE FOOD 5·1 kg

5 WORM FOOD 2·6 kg

6 HIPPO FOOD 3·7 kg

7 SNAKE BITES 4·6 kg

8 LION CUB NIBBLES 5·4 kg

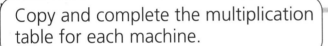

Copy and complete the multiplication table for each machine.

9.

in	1·2	2·3	3·5		
out	6·0				

in	1·2	2·3	3·5	7·5	8·4
out					

9 1·2 in ×5 out 6·0

10 in ×7 out

11 in ×8 out

Explore

Use number cards 2, 3, 4 and 5.

Make a decimal multiplication using 3 cards.

What is the nearest answer you can make to 10, 12, 14, 16, 18, 20?

3 4 5

3·4 × 5

Copy and complete.

1   85 ÷ 5   2   96 ÷ 4   3   81 ÷ 3

4   95 ÷ 5   5   96 ÷ 6   6   75 ÷ 5

7   91 ÷ 7   8   92 ÷ 4   9   105 ÷ 7

1.
```
        1 5
      8 5
   -  5 0      1 0 × 5
      3 5
   -  3 5        7 × 5
        0
```
85 ÷ 5 = 17

Write how many children in each team.

10   105 children in 3 teams

10.
```
        3 5
    1 0 5
   -   9 0      3 0 × 3
      1 5
   -  1 5        5 × 3
        0
```
105 ÷ 3 = 35

11   116 children in 4 teams

12   145 children in 5 teams

13   176 children in 4 teams

14   156 children in 6 teams

15   196 children in 7 teams

16   176 children in 8 teams

17   185 children in 5 teams

18   132 children in 6 teams

e   Write how many children are left over if there are 9 teams each time.

Dividing

There are 9 strings on a puppet.

Write how many puppets can be made and how many strings are left over.

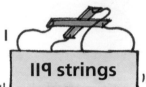

1 119 strings

I.   ⎡1 2⎤

```
   1 1 9
 −   9 0        1 0 × 9
     2 9
 −   2 7        3 × 9
       2
```

1 1 9 ÷ 9 = 1 3 r 2
1 3 puppets,
2 strings left

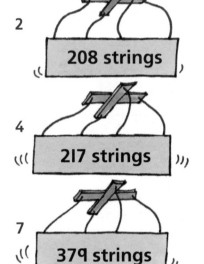

2 208 strings

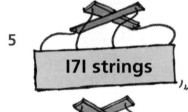

3 191 strings

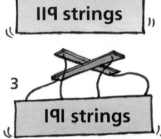

4 217 strings

5 171 strings

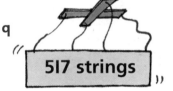

6 220 strings

7 379 strings

8 460 strings

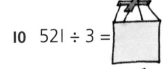

9 517 strings

Copy and complete.

10 521 ÷ 3 =

11 278 ÷ 5 =

12 416 ÷ 3 =

13 372 ÷ 6 =

14 619 ÷ 4 =

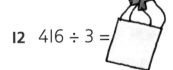

15 832 ÷ 7 =

16 927 ÷ 8 =

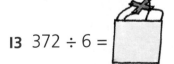

I0.   ⎡2 0 0⎤

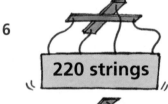

```
   5 2 1
 −3 0 0        1 0 0 × 3
   2 2 1
 −1 5 0         5 0 × 3
     7 1
 −  6 0         2 0 × 3
     1 1
 −    9          3 × 3
      2
```

5 2 1 ÷ 3 = 1 7 3 r 2

38

There are 6 stickers in a packet.

Write how many are left over.

1
104 stickers

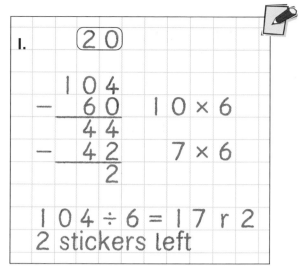

I. ⟨2 0⟩

```
    1 0 4
 −    6 0    1 0 × 6
      4 4
 −    4 2    7 × 6
       2
```

$104 ÷ 6 = 17 \text{ r } 2$
2 stickers left

2
203 stickers

3
736 stickers

4
819 stickers

5
447 stickers

6
256 stickers

7
316 stickers

8
732 stickers

q
860 stickers

Problems

10 A robot in a factory sews buttons on coats. Each coat has **7** buttons.

The robot breaks down after sewing **328** buttons.

How many coats are finished?

How many more buttons are needed to finish the last coat?

11 There are **5** children with paper rounds. The newsagent has **747** papers to deliver.

Each child takes an equal number of papers. How many does each deliver? How many are left for the newsagent to deliver?

The newsagent pays **8p** for every paper the children deliver. How much does he pay each child?

Copy and complete.

1 $64 \div 3 =$

2 $59 \div 6 =$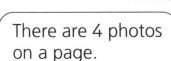

3 $71 \div 5 =$

4 $82 \div 7 =$

5 $74 \div 8 =$

6 $87 \div 3 =$

7 $97 \div 6 =$

8 $89 \div 5 =$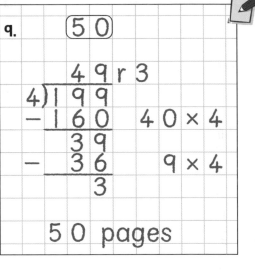

I. $\boxed{2\;0}$

```
      2 1 r 1
  3 ) 6 4
    - 6 0      2 0 × 3
        4
    -   3      1 × 3
        1
```

There are 4 photos on a page.

How many pages for each set?

9. $\boxed{5\;0}$

```
      4 9 r 3
  4 ) 1 9 9
    - 1 6 0      4 0 × 4
        3 9
    -   3 6      9 × 4
          3

      5 0  pages
```

9 **199 photos**

10 **371 photos**

11 **159 photos**

12 **161 photos**

13 **385 photos**

14 **173 photos**

15 **255 photos**

16 **289 photos**

17 **377 photos**

18 **267 photos**

e How many pages are needed if there are 6 photos on a page?

Oil lamps are packed in boxes of 7.

Write how many full boxes there are and how many lamps are left over.

I. 3 0

```
        2 8 r 1
    7)1 9 7
    - 1 4 0      2 0 × 7
        5 7
    -   5 6      8 × 7
          1
```

2 8 boxes, 1 lamp left

1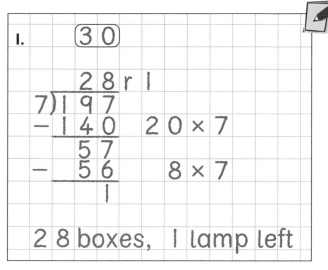
197 lamps

2
115 lamps

3
296 lamps

4
156 lamps

5
189 lamps

6
227 lamps

7
305 lamps

8
353 lamps

ⓔ How many are left over if lamps are packed in boxes of 9?

Each oil drum holds 1 gallon of oil.

Write how many drums are needed.

9
207 pints

9. 2 5

```
        2 5 r 7
    8)2 0 7
    - 1 6 0      2 0 × 8
        4 7
    -   4 0      5 × 8
          7
```

2 6 drums needed

10
104 pints

11
219 pints

12
117 pints

13
333 pints

I gallon = 8 pints

14
197 pints

15
257 pints

16
339 pints

Remainders

The children ride on the big wheel in sixes.

How many full cars are there? How many are needed altogether?

I.
```
        (3 5)

        3 4 r I
   6)2 0 5
   - 1 8 0      30 × 6
       2 5
   -   2 4      4 × 6
         1
```

3 4 full cars
3 5 cars needed

1

205 children

2

337 children

3

217 children

4

251 children

5

341 children

6

278 children

7

457 children

8

310 children

9

519 children

10

634 children

11

561 children

Explore

Divide 100 by 9.

Divide 200 by 9.

Divide 300 by 9.

Continue for 400, 500, …

What do you notice? Write about any patterns.

Rounding

Write the position of each arrow.

Round to the nearest whole number.

1. $a = 3.2 \rightarrow 3$

Remember 0·5 rounds up to 1.

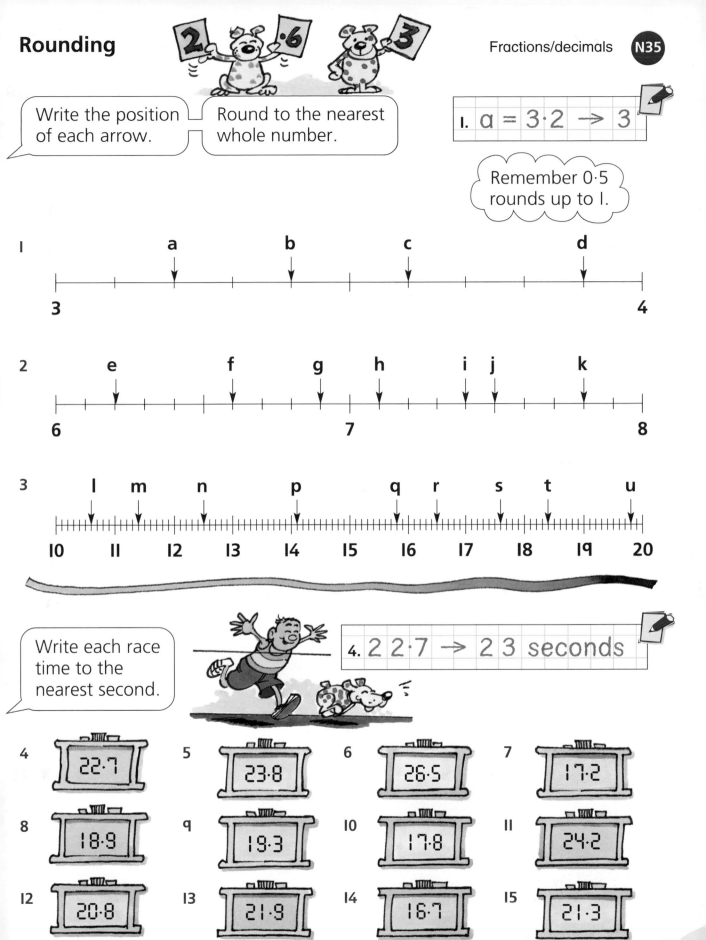

1
a   b   c   d
3 4

2
e   f   g   h   i   j   k
6 .... 7 8

3
l   m   n   p   q   r   s   t   u
10 11 12 13 14 15 16 17 18 19 20

Write each race time to the nearest second.

4. $22.7 \rightarrow 23$ seconds

4. 22·7

5. 23·8

6. 26·5

7. 17·2

8. 18·9

9. 19·3

10. 17·8

11. 24·2

12. 20·8

13. 21·9

14. 16·7

15. 21·3

Rounding

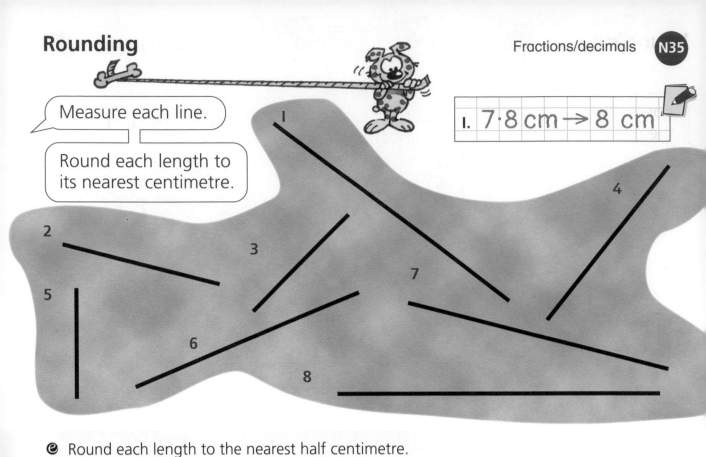

Measure each line.

Round each length to its nearest centimetre.

1. 7·8 cm → 8 cm

e Round each length to the nearest half centimetre.

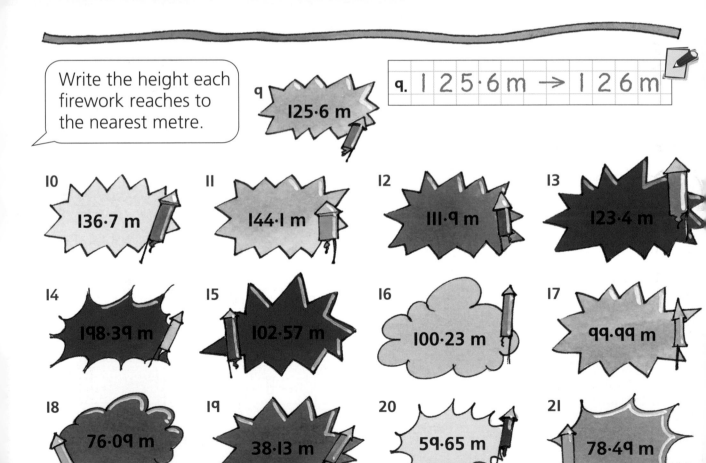

Write the height each firework reaches to the nearest metre.

9. 125·6 m → 126 m

9 125·6 m

10 136·7 m

11 144·1 m

12 111·9 m

13 123·4 m

14 198·39 m

15 102·57 m

16 100·23 m

17 99·99 m

18 76·09 m

19 38·13 m

20 59·65 m

21 78·49 m

Rounding

Round each price to the nearest pound.

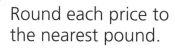

1  £11·93

 1. £11·93 → £12

2 £12·17

3 £13·29

4 £14·79

5 £10·19

6 £12·55

7 £13·21

8 £12·79

9 £12·91

e Round each price to the nearest ten pence.

Explore

Use the number cards shown.

Use the cards to make decimal numbers, e.g. 2·4, 3·2, …

Write their nearest whole numbers.

2·4 → 2

3·2 → 3

How many different decimal numbers can you make?

How many different nearest whole numbers can you find?

Adding decimals

Each snake grows to be 1 m long.

Write how much more each snake grows.

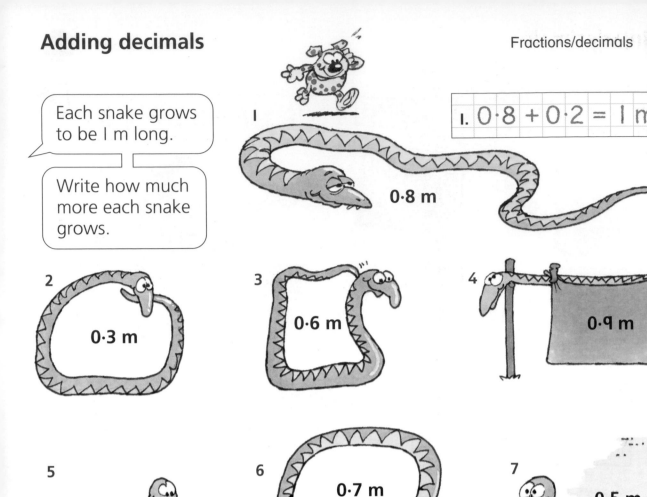

1

0·8 m

1. $0·8 + 0·2 = 1$ m

2

0·3 m

3

0·6 m

4

0·9 m

5

0·2 m

6

0·7 m

7

0·5 m

e The snakes were 0·1 m long when they were born. How much has each grown?

Copy and complete.

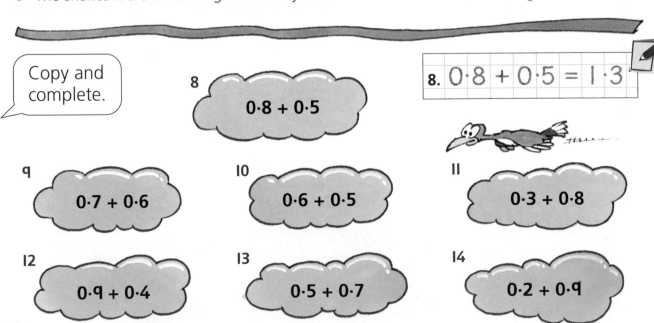

8

0·8 + 0·5

8. $0·8 + 0·5 = 1·3$

9

0·7 + 0·6

10

0·6 + 0·5

11

0·3 + 0·8

12

0·9 + 0·4

13

0·5 + 0·7

14

0·2 + 0·9

Adding decimals

Write how much water is in each tank.

1. $5.8 + 3.5 = 9.3$ l

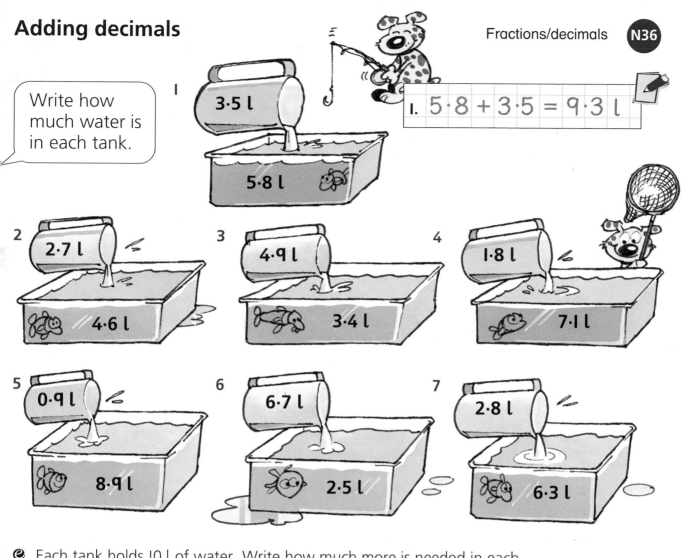

1. **3.5 l** / **5.8 l**

2. **2.7 l** / **4.6 l**

3. **4.9 l** / **3.4 l**

4. **1.8 l** / **7.1 l**

5. **0.9 l** / **8.9 l**

6. **6.7 l** / **2.5 l**

7. **2.8 l** / **6.3 l**

ℯ Each tank holds 10 l of water. Write how much more is needed in each.

Write the total cost of the fish and chips and the ice cream.

8. £3.49 + £2.70 = £6.19

8. **£3.49** **£2.70**

9. **£3.38** **£1.91**

10. **£4.46** **£2.72**

11. **£3.87** **£1.32**

12. **£3.55** **£2.64**

13. **£4.29** **£2.90**

14. **£3.74** **£1.55**

47

Subtracting decimals

There are 2 routes to each school.

Write the difference between the long route and the short cut.

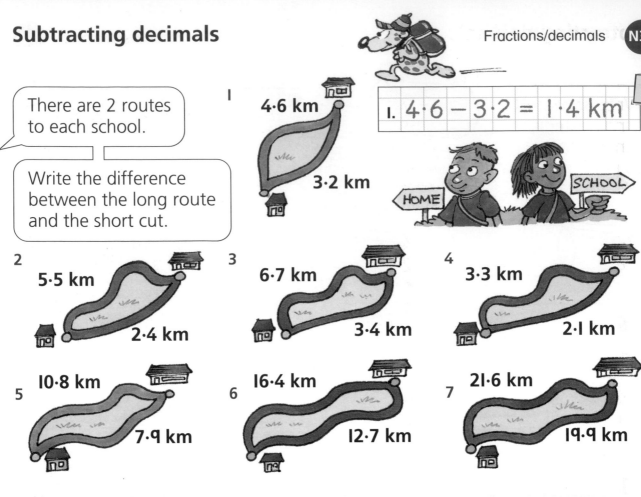

1

4·6 km

3·2 km

HOME   SCHOOL

1. $4·6 - 3·2 = 1·4$ km

2

5·5 km

2·4 km

3

6·7 km

3·4 km

4

3·3 km

2·1 km

5

10·8 km

7·9 km

6

16·4 km

12·7 km

7

21·6 km

19·9 km

◉ Find how much is saved in a week by taking the short cut to each school every day.

Each moped uses some petrol.

Write how much is left.

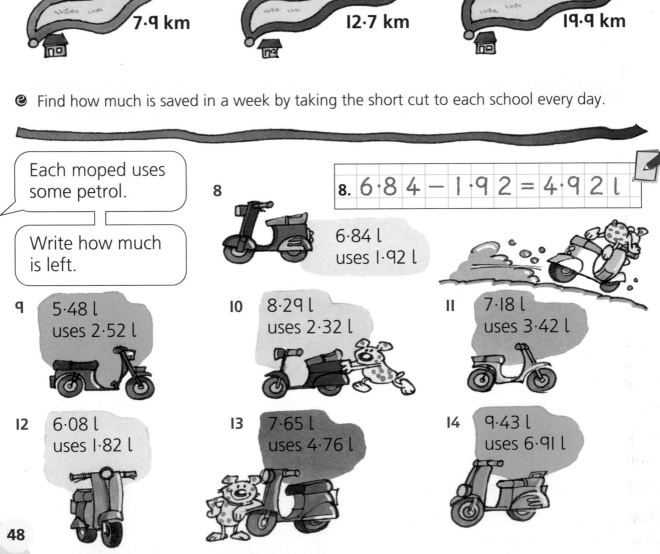

8

6·84 l
uses 1·92 l

8. $6·84 - 1·92 = 4·92$ l

9

5·48 l
uses 2·52 l

10

8·29 l
uses 2·32 l

11

7·18 l
uses 3·42 l

12

6·08 l
uses 1·82 l

13

7·65 l
uses 4·76 l

14

9·43 l
uses 6·91 l

Subtracting decimals

Write how much further each runner must go to reach home.

I

1. $4 \cdot 64 - 1 \cdot 72 = 2 \cdot 92$ km

4·64 km

1·72 km

2   3·26 km
    1·81 km

3   4·71 km
    2·34 km

4   5·18 km
    3·62 km

5   7·31 km
    5·68 km

6   4·29 km
    1·73 km

7   6·83 km
    4·69 km

8   13·65 km
    10·75 km

9   10·85 km
    9·16 km

10   20·46 km
     7·98 km

ℯ Round each answer to its nearest kilometre.

Explore

Use number cards 1 to 9.

Make 2 decimal numbers (units, tenths, hundredths).

Find the difference between them.

How many subtractions like this can you find with the answer 1·23?

☐ . ☐ ☐ — ☐ . ☐ ☐

9·76 − 8·53 = 1·23

Percentages

Write what percentage of each grid is red, blue and yellow.

1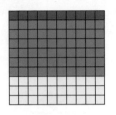

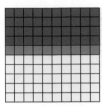

1. red → 5 0 %
blue → 4 0 %
yellow → 1 0 %

2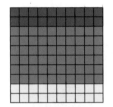

3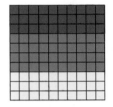

4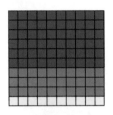

5

6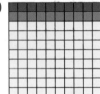

7

8

9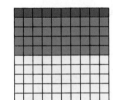

10

11

12

13

Write each percentage in hundredths and then in tenths.

14 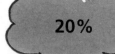 30%

14. $30\% = \dfrac{30}{100} = \dfrac{3}{10}$

15 90%

16 60%

17 10%

18 50%

19 80%

20 20%

21 40%

22 70%

50

Percentages

Write what percentage of each grid is blue.

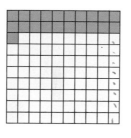

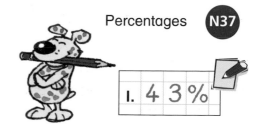

1. 4 3 %

2   3   4   5

6   7   8   q

Write what percentage of each grid is yellow.

1a. 5 7 %

Write each fraction as a percentage.

10   $\frac{48}{100}$

10. 4 8 %

11   $\frac{38}{100}$ 12 $\frac{92}{100}$ 13 $\frac{40}{100}$ 14 $\frac{21}{100}$ 15 $\frac{5}{100}$

Write each percentage as a fraction.

16   29%

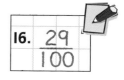

16. $\frac{29}{100}$

17   10%   18   98%   19   75%   20   67%   21   2%

Percentages

Write what percentage of each grid is green.

I. 2 5 %

Use this 10 × 10 grid to help you.

1
2
3

4
5
6

7
8
9
10

Write each fraction as a percentage.

II. 5 0 %

11 $\frac{1}{2}$

12 $\frac{1}{4}$

13 $\frac{3}{4}$

14 $\frac{1}{10}$

15 $\frac{1}{5}$

16 $\frac{3}{5}$

17 $\frac{7}{10}$

18 $\frac{1}{20}$

19 $\frac{17}{20}$

Percentages

> Each price goes down by 50%.

> Write the new prices.

I. 50% of $80p = 40p$

1

80p

2

60p

3
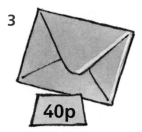
40p

4
Phone Jim
50p

5

90p

6

70p

7

20p

8
£1

9
66p

10

84p

11

46p

12

36p

@ Each old price goes up by 50%. Write the new prices.

Explore

Throw a dice 25 times and record the results.

What percentage of the throws were 1s, 2s, 3s, …?

Making I and IO

Write the pair to make I.

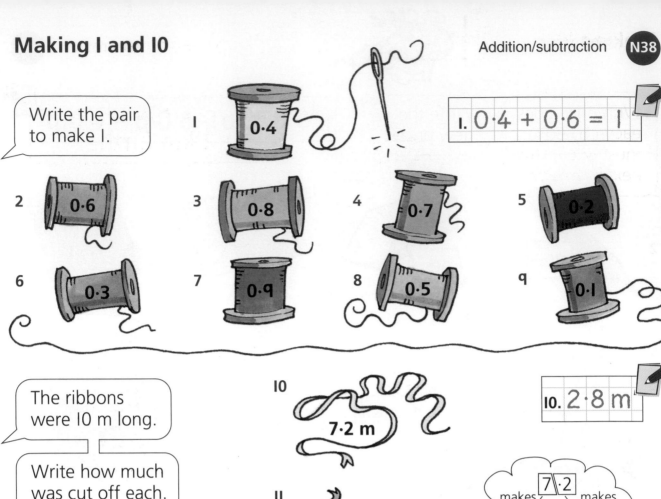

I

1. $0.4 + 0.6 = 1$

2 0·6

3 0·8

4 0·7

5 0·2

6 0·3

7 0·9

8 0·5

q 0·1

The ribbons were IO m long.

Write how much was cut off each.

IO. 2·8 m

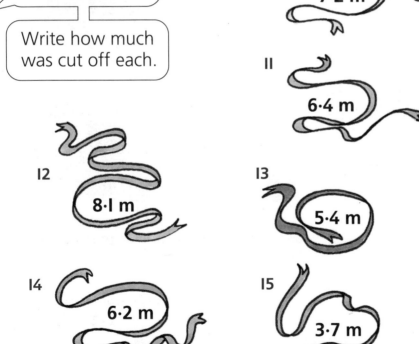

IO 7·2 m

II 6·4 m

makes IO   7 | ·2   makes I

3   ·8

– I

2 | ·8

I2 8·1 m

I3 5·4 m

I4 6·2 m

I5 3·7 m

I6 4·6 m

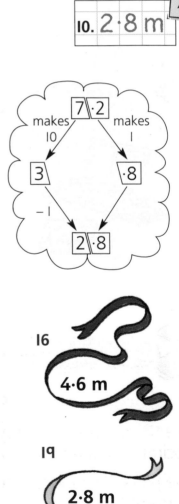

I7 2·5 m

I8 3·3 m

I9 2·8 m

e Write the lengths in order.

Making 10

Write how far each cyclist must ride to the next kilometre.

I

2·8 km

I. $2·8 + 0·2 = 3$ km
0·2 km further

2

7·4 km

3

8·6 km

4

6·3 km

5

3·5 km

6

5·9 km

7

4·2 km

8

5·8 km

9

6·6 km

10
2·7 km

ℯ How many more kilometres to reach 10 km?

Explore

Use number cards 0 to 9.

Use the cards to make two decimal numbers (units and tenths).

The pairs of numbers must add to make 10.

How many pairs can you find?

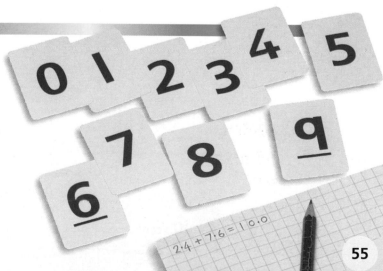

2·4 + 7·6 = 10.0

Write how much change from £10·00.

1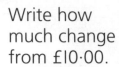

£3·40

1. £ 1 0·0 0 – £ 3·4 0 = £ 6·6 0

2  £8·70

3 £6·50

4  £8·40

5  £2·20

6 £5·10

7 £1·90

8 £3·60

9 £7·50

10 £4·20

Problems

11 The balloon rises **1·3 m** from the ground.

It goes up another **2·5 m**.

How much further must it rise to reach **10 m**?

12 The crab is at **4·7 m** below the surface of the sea.

It rises **2·1 m**.

How far must it sink to be **10 m** below the surface?

Adding decimals

Copy and complete.

Estimate first.

1.
```
   8
  4·8 5
+ 3·2 5
 ‾‾‾‾‾‾
  8·1 0
  ₁ ₁
```

1
```
  4·8 5
+ 3·2 5
‾‾‾‾‾‾‾
```

2
```
  1·8 4
+ 2·2 8
‾‾‾‾‾‾‾
```

3
```
  5·9 1
+ 1·8 6
‾‾‾‾‾‾‾
```

4
```
  1 2·7
+ 1 7·5
‾‾‾‾‾‾‾
```

5
```
  5·9 1
+ 2·8 4
‾‾‾‾‾‾‾
```

6
```
  2 1·6
+ 4 3·7
‾‾‾‾‾‾‾
```

7
```
  6·2 7
+ 1·8 5
‾‾‾‾‾‾‾
```

8
```
  8·0 9
+ 2·7 6
‾‾‾‾‾‾‾
```

9
```
  6 5·4
+ 3 9·3
‾‾‾‾‾‾‾
```

10
```
  4·7 7
+ 5·4 8
‾‾‾‾‾‾‾
```

11
```
  4 6·8
+ 5 9·7
‾‾‾‾‾‾‾
```

Write the cost of the items for each party.

12

£4·24

£3·46

£5·81

12.
```
£ 1 2·5 0
  £ 4·2 4
  £ 3·4 6
  £ 5·8 1
£ 1 3·5 1
    ₁ ₁
```

13

£2·79

£1·99

£4·86

14

£3·87

£5·23

£6·16

15

£7·44

£4·95

£2·09

16

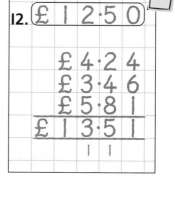

£5·63

£5·19

£7·52

17

£8·49

£1·99

£4·99

ℯ How much change would you get from a £20 note for each party?

Adding decimals

Each child swims 3 lengths.

Write the total times.

1 **Sally**

34·5 seconds	28·5 seconds	36·3 seconds

```
  3 4·5
  2 8·5
+ 3 6·3
  9 9·3   seconds
  1 1
```

I. 1 0 0 seconds

2 **Ahmed**

39·6 seconds	41·8 seconds	44·4 seconds

3 **Jake**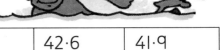

45·6 seconds	35·8 seconds	34·2 seconds

4 **Mel**

43·1 seconds	45·2 seconds	42·9 seconds

5 **Parvati**

37·9 seconds	36·3 seconds	40·4 seconds

6 **Jennie**

35·9 seconds	39·8 seconds	40·3 seconds

7 **Wes**

44·8 seconds	42·6 seconds	41·9 seconds

e Each child swims a fourth length in 41·6 seconds. Write the total times.

Explore

Use number cards 1 to 9.

Use them to make three decimal numbers (units, tenths and hundredths).

Add the decimals together.

What is the nearest total to 10 you can find?

Adding decimals

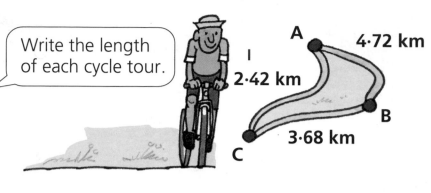

Write the length of each cycle tour.

A   4·72 km

I   2·42 km

B

C   3·68 km

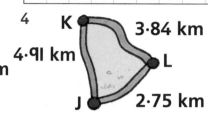

1.   [1 1 km]

```
        4 · 7 2
    +   3 · 6 8
        2 · 4 2
      1 0 · 8 2   km
        1 1
```

2

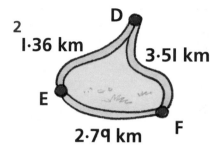

D

1·36 km   3·51 km

E

F   2·79 km

3

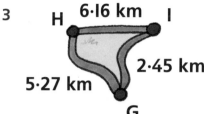

H   6·16 km   I

5·27 km   2·45 km

G

4

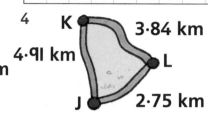

K   3·84 km

4·91 km   L

J   2·75 km

5

M   5·08 km

N

4·36 km   3·29 km

P

6

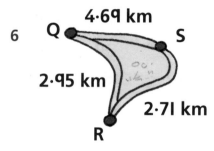

Q   4·69 km   S

2·95 km   2·71 km

R

7

T   2·66 km   U

4·41 km   6·82 km

V

 How much further must each cyclist ride to reach 15 km?

Problems

8 Chloe has **£3·69** in her money box.

She buys a magazine for **£2·99**.

She earns **£6·99** cleaning windows.

How much does she have now?

How much more must she save to have **£10**?

q The Jackson family is going on holiday.

They have 3 suitcases which weigh **10·73 kg**, **15·4 kg** and **18·28 kg**.

The weight limit is **40 kg**. How much over the limit are they?

Copy and complete.

1. $1000 - 27 = 973$

1 $1000 - 27 = $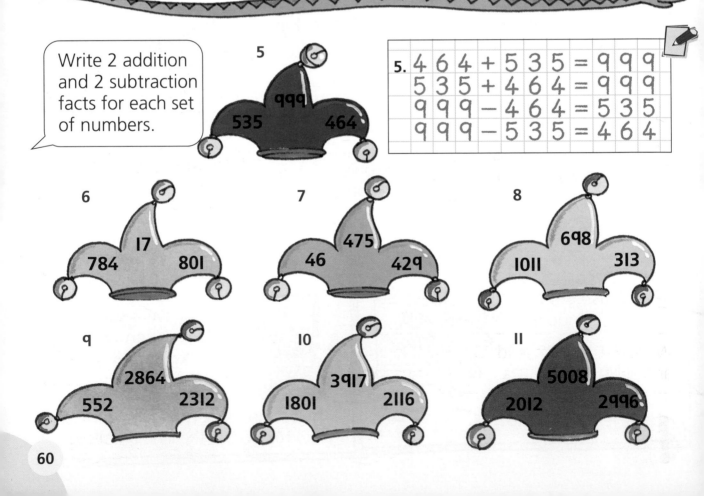

$27 + $ 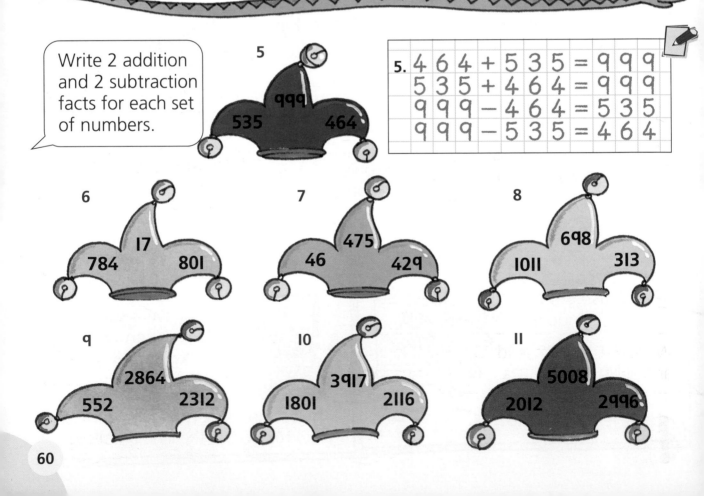 $= 1000$

$1000 - $ 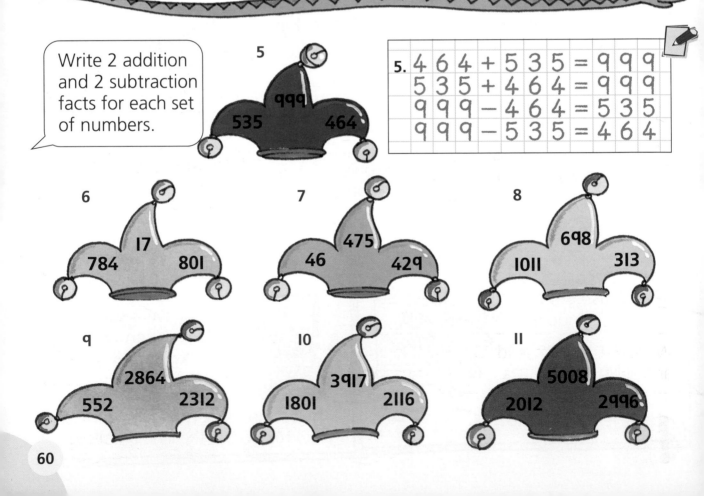 $= 27$

2 $3000 - 899 = $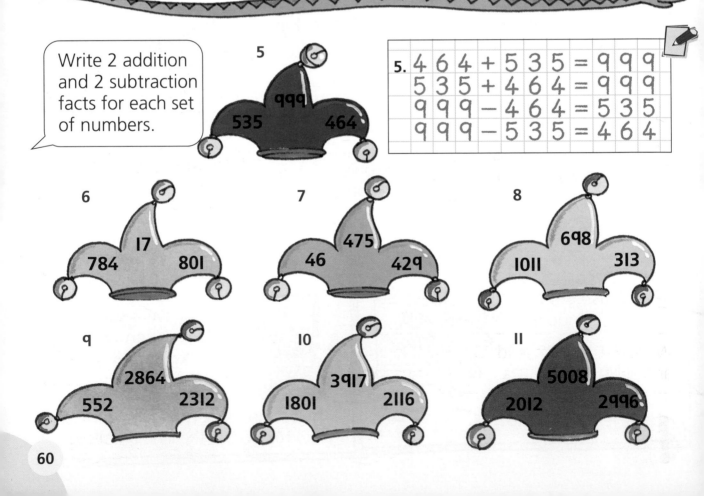

$899 + $ $= 3000$

$3000 - $ $= 899$

3 $4000 - 1501 = $

$1501 + $ $= 4000$

$4000 - $ $= 1501$

4 $2004 - 699 = $

$699 + $ $= 2004$

$2004 - $ $= 699$

℮ Write some more sets of related addition and subtraction facts.

Write 2 addition and 2 subtraction facts for each set of numbers.

5 999 535 464

5.
$464 + 535 = 999$
$535 + 464 = 999$
$999 - 464 = 535$
$999 - 535 = 464$

6 17 784 801

7 475 46 429

8 698 1011 313

9 2864 552 2312

10 3917 1801 2116

11 5008 2012 2996

60

Deriving related facts

$$475 - 389 = 86$$

$$389 + 475 = 864$$

$$290 - 145 = 145$$

$$290 + 145 = 435$$

$$1012 - 29 = 983$$

$$29 + 1012 = 1041$$

$$345 + 543 = 888$$

$$543 - 345 = 198$$

1 What is the difference between 475 and 864?

2 What is 983 subtracted from 1012?

3 What is 543 taken from 888?

4 What is the total of 475 and 389?

Use the facts above to help you.

5 What is half of 290?

6 What is 475 more than 389?

7 What is the difference between 543 and 345?

8 What is 29 more than 1012?

9 What is 345 more than 543?

10 What is double 145?

Write 10 different addition and subtraction facts.

Use only these numbers.

 538
 1000
 462
 319
 143
 8
 311

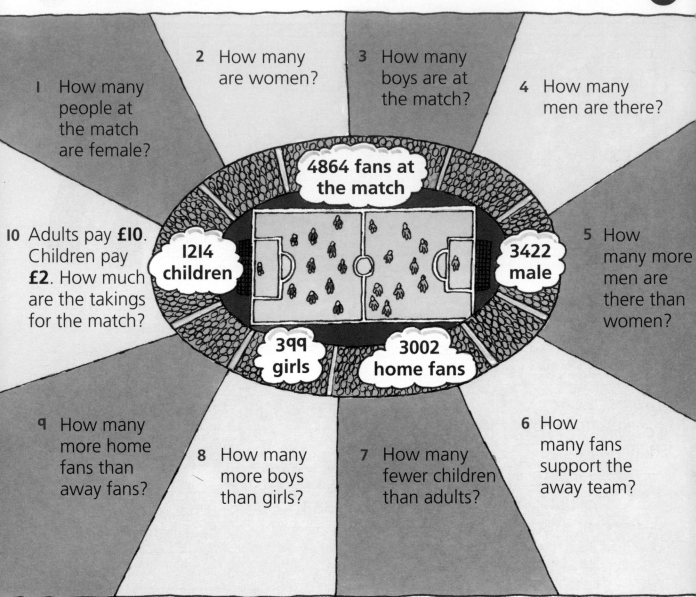

1 How many people at the match are female?

2 How many are women?

3 How many boys are at the match?

4 How many men are there?

4864 fans at the match

1214 children

3422 male

399 girls

3002 home fans

5 How many more men are there than women?

6 How many fans support the away team?

7 How many fewer children than adults?

8 How many more boys than girls?

9 How many more home fans than away fans?

10 Adults pay **£10**. Children pay **£2**. How much are the takings for the match?

Explore

Write a 3-digit number, e.g. 104.

Find its digital root by adding its digits until you get a 1-digit number. Multiply this number by 8.

Add the answer to the 3-digit number. Find the digital root of the total.

Repeat for other 3-digit numbers.

What do you notice?

Subtracting decimals

Copy and complete.

1.
$$
\begin{array}{r}
4\,2\cdot3 \\
-\ 2\,6\cdot4 \\
\hline
\end{array}
$$

1. $\boxed{1\ 5}$

$$
\begin{array}{r}
{}^{3}\!\!\not{4}\,{}^{1}\!2\cdot{}^{1}3 \\
-\ 2\ 6\cdot4 \\
\hline
1\ 5\cdot9
\end{array}
$$

2.
$$
\begin{array}{r}
5\,2\cdot3 \\
-\ 3\,6\cdot9 \\
\hline
\end{array}
$$

3.
$$
\begin{array}{r}
4\,3\cdot3 \\
-\ 2\,5\cdot8 \\
\hline
\end{array}
$$

4.
$$
\begin{array}{r}
3\,1\cdot2 \\
-\ 1\,4\cdot3 \\
\hline
\end{array}
$$

5.
$$
\begin{array}{r}
7\,4\cdot5 \\
-\ 5\,7\cdot6 \\
\hline
\end{array}
$$

6.
$$
\begin{array}{r}
5\,1\cdot7 \\
-\ 3\,9\cdot8 \\
\hline
\end{array}
$$

7.
$$
\begin{array}{r}
6\,2\cdot4 \\
-\ 1\,9\cdot8 \\
\hline
\end{array}
$$

Write the difference between the cost of a child's and an adult's ticket.

8

CHILD £2·60

ADULT £3·12

8. $\boxed{\pounds\ 0\cdot5\ 0}$

$$
\begin{array}{r}
\pounds\ {}^{2}\!\not{3}\cdot{}^{1}1\ 2 \\
-\ \pounds\ 2\cdot6\ 0 \\
\hline
\pounds\ 0\cdot5\ 2 = 5\,2\,\text{p}
\end{array}
$$

9
CHILD £1·89

ADULT £3·14

10
ADULT £5·12

CHILD £4·24

11
ADULT £7·12

CHILD £4·68

12
CHILD £5·49

ADULT £9·20

13
ADULT £3·70

CHILD £2·99

14
CHILD £4·83

ADULT £6·42

ℯ Find the difference between the cost of two children's tickets and one adult's ticket.

Subtracting decimals

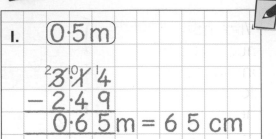

Write the difference between the lengths of the rockets.

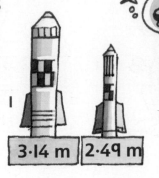

1   3·14 m   2·49 m

1.   0·5 m

$$\begin{array}{r} {}^{2}\cancel{3}{}^{10}\cancel{1}{}^{1}4 \\ -\ 2\cdot4\ 9 \\ \hline 0\cdot6\ 5\,m = 6\ 5\ cm \end{array}$$

2   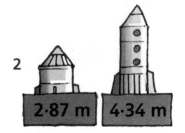   2·87 m   4·34 m

3   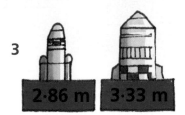   2·86 m   3·33 m

4   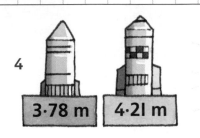   3·78 m   4·21 m

5   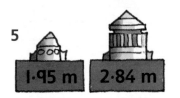   1·95 m   2·84 m

6   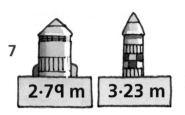   1·76 m   2·53 m

7   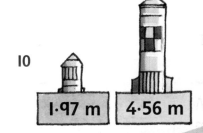   2·79 m   3·23 m

8   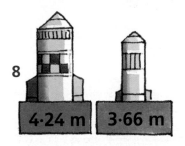   4·24 m   3·66 m

9   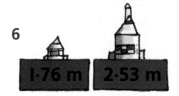   1·78 m   3·04 m

10      1·97 m   4·56 m

Explore

Use number cards 1 to 9.

Make three decimal numbers (units, tenths and hundredths) using each card just once.

Subtract the numbers from 20.

What is the nearest answer to 0 you can find?

Subtracting decimals

Write how much longer one length of cloth is than the other.

1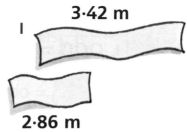

3·42 m

2·86 m

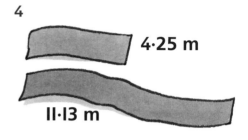

1. $\boxed{0.5\,m}$

$$
\begin{array}{r}
^2\cancel{3}\cdot^{13}\cancel{4}\,^1\cancel{2} \\
-\ 2\cdot 8\ 6 \\
\hline
0\cdot 5\ 6\ m = 5\ 6\ cm
\end{array}
$$

2 10·98 m

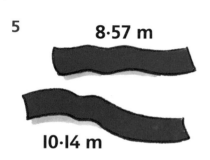

6·16 m

3 5·17 m

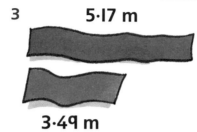

3·49 m

4

4·25 m

11·13 m

5 8·57 m

10·14 m

6 6·82 m

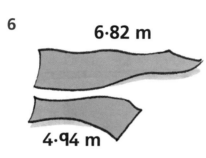

4·94 m

7 9·61 m

7·83 m

e The pieces of cloth are cut from rolls of 20 m. How much is left on each roll?

---

8 Wai Lin has **£10** in her purse.

She eats a hamburger and fries which cost **£4·63**. She buys a cinema ticket for **£2·48**.

How much is in her purse now?

Problems

9 Peaches the poodle is overweight. She weighs **24·7 kg**.

She loses **1·64 kg** in one month, then **1·78 kg** the next month.

How much does she weigh now?

10 In the cola-drinking competition each team has **5 l** of cola to drink.

COLA

Ali drinks **1·73 l**, Jade drinks **1·28 l** and Sol drinks **1·46 l**.

Do they finish the cola? If not, how much is left?

Mixed problems

1

Think of a number …

… double it …

… add 30 …

… halve it …

… subtract 1 from the tens digit.

Try this with 4 different numbers.

2

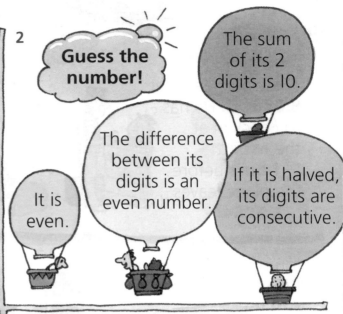

Guess the number!

The sum of its 2 digits is 10.

The difference between its digits is an even number.

It is even.

If it is halved, its digits are consecutive.

3

I am less than 1000 and greater than 100.

My first and last digits are the same.

Who am I?

I am divisible by 2, 3 and 4 without leaving a remainder.

4

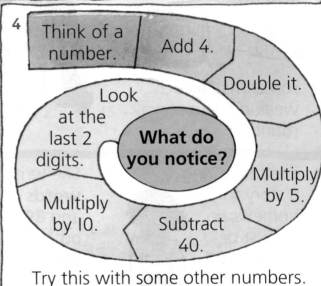

Think of a number.

Add 4.

Double it.

Multiply by 5.

Subtract 40.

Multiply by 10.

Look at the last 2 digits.

What do you notice?

Try this with some other numbers.

5

Think of a number.

Add your age.

Multiply by 4.

Halve it.

Take away twice the number you first thought of.

Halve again.

What do you notice about the answer?

6

Guess the number.

It is less than $\frac{1}{2}$ and greater than $\frac{1}{4}$.

It has 2 digits after the decimal point.

The digits add to 13.